Balancing Balls

▶ Take away one ball each time.

$$3 - 1 = \boxed{2}$$

$$5 - 1 = \boxed{}$$

$$4 - 1 = \boxed{}$$

$$2 - 1 = \boxed{}$$

$$1 - 1 = \boxed{}$$

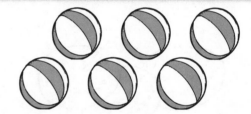

$$6 - 1 = \boxed{}$$

▶ Write the number that is one less.

$\boxed{4}$ 5	$\boxed{}$ 1	6
$\boxed{}$ 2	$\boxed{}$ 4	3

Beginning Subtraction Facts • LL 6929

Otter Do It

▶ How many are left?

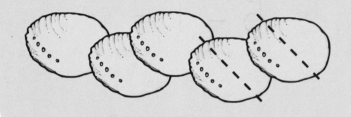
$$5 - 2 = 3$$

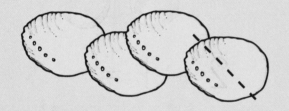
☐ – ☐ = ☐

☐ – ☐ = ☐

☐ – ☐ = ☐

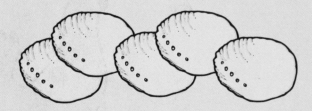
☐ – ☐ = ☐

Beginning Subtraction Facts • LL 6929

▶ Find the answer.

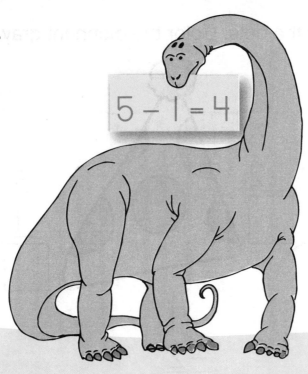

$5 - 1 = 4$

$5 - 5 = \boxed{}$ $5 - 3 = \boxed{}$

$4 - 1 = \boxed{}$ $4 - 2 = \boxed{}$

$4 - 2 = \boxed{}$ $2 - 0 = \boxed{}$

$3 - 3 = \boxed{}$ $3 - 2 = \boxed{}$

$2 - 1 = \boxed{}$ $5 - 4 = \boxed{}$

$4 - 0 = \boxed{}$ $3 - 1 = \boxed{}$

Elmer's Birthday

▶ Start at **0**. Connect the dots. Color the elephant gray.

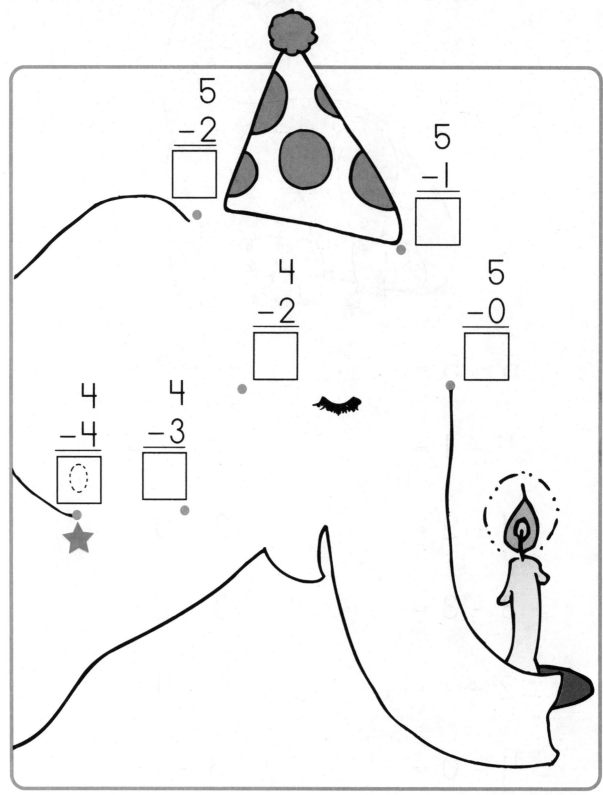

$$\begin{array}{r} 5 \\ -2 \\ \hline \end{array}$$

$$\begin{array}{r} 5 \\ -1 \\ \hline \end{array}$$

$$\begin{array}{r} 4 \\ -2 \\ \hline \end{array}$$

$$\begin{array}{r} 5 \\ -0 \\ \hline \end{array}$$

$$\begin{array}{r} 4 \\ -4 \\ \hline \end{array}$$

$$\begin{array}{r} 4 \\ -3 \\ \hline \end{array}$$

Beginning Subtraction Facts • LL 6929

▶ Can you find the answer?

```
    4            5            3
  - 3          - 1          - 1
  [   ]        [   ]        [   ]

    3            3            5
  - 0          - 2          - 2
  [   ]        [   ]        [   ]

    1            5            4
  - 1          - 4          - 1
  [   ]        [   ]        [   ]

    4            2            3
  - 2          - 1          - 3
  [   ]        [   ]        [   ]

    2            4            5
  - 2          - 1          - 3
  [   ]        [   ]        [   ]
```

Lots of Lambs

▶ Draw lines to match the numbers.

4 – 3 = ⋮

1 – 1 =

2 – 1 =

3 – 2 =

3 – 3 =

5 – 4 =

5 – 5 =

2 – 2 =

3 – 1 =

3 – 0 =

4 – 1 =

5 – 3 =

5 – 2 =

4 – 2 =

Beginning Subtraction Facts • LL 6929

How many fish are left?

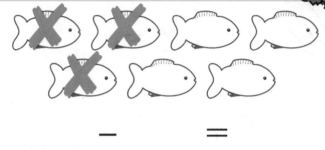

_____ — _____ = _____

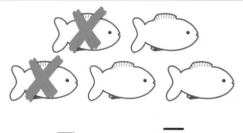

_____ — _____ = _____

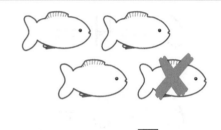

_____ — _____ = _____

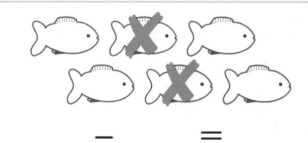

_____ — _____ = _____

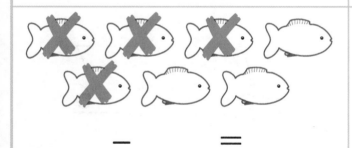

_____ — _____ = _____

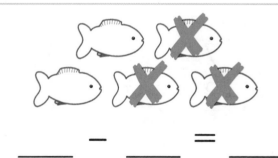

_____ — _____ = _____

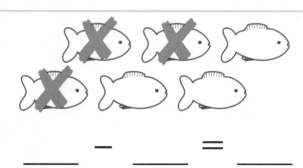

_____ — _____ = _____

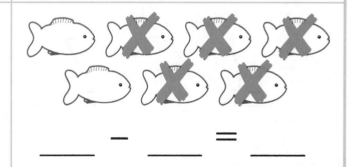

_____ — _____ = _____

Beginning Subtraction Facts • LL 6929

Review

Find the difference.

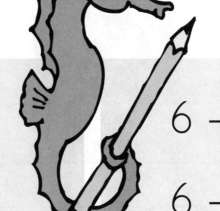

5 − 4 = ☐

5 − 1 = ☐

5 − 3 = ☐

5 − 0 = ☐

5 − 5 = ☐

6 − 5 = ☐

6 − 2 = ☐

6 − 1 = ☐

6 − 4 = ☐

6 − 3 = ☐

$$\begin{array}{r} 7 \\ -3 \\ \hline \end{array}$$ ☐

$$\begin{array}{r} 7 \\ -2 \\ \hline \end{array}$$ ☐

$$\begin{array}{r} 7 \\ -5 \\ \hline \end{array}$$ ☐

$$\begin{array}{r} 7 \\ -6 \\ \hline \end{array}$$ ☐

$$\begin{array}{r} 7 \\ -4 \\ \hline \end{array}$$ ☐

$$\begin{array}{r} 7 \\ -7 \\ \hline \end{array}$$ ☐

$$\begin{array}{r} 7 \\ -1 \\ \hline \end{array}$$ ☐

$$\begin{array}{r} 7 \\ -0 \\ \hline \end{array}$$ ☐

▶ How fast can you find the answer?

7 −4	2 −0	4 −2	3 −3	7 −1	5 −2
6 −2	5 −3	5 −5	7 −5	4 −3	2 −1
3 −1	5 −4	7 −2	5 −1	3 −2	4 −4
5 −0	6 −6	4 −2	3 −2	6 −0	5 −0
6 −5	7 −6	6 −4	5 −3	4 −3	6 −1

Watermelon Seeds

 How many are left?

9 — 7 = 2

_____ — _____ = _____

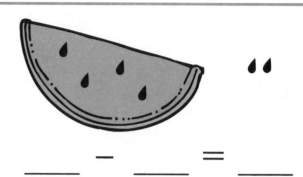

_____ — _____ = _____

_____ — _____ = _____

_____ — _____ = _____

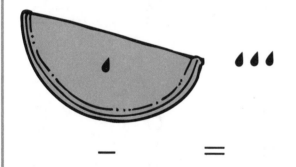

_____ — _____ = _____

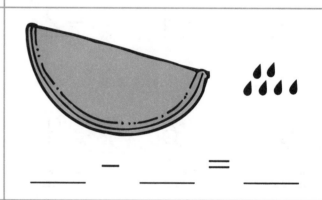

_____ — _____ = _____

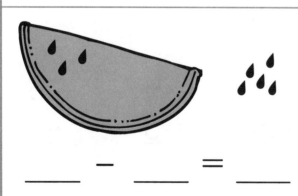

_____ — _____ = _____

_____ — _____ = _____

Hungry Caterpillar

▶ How many did I eat?

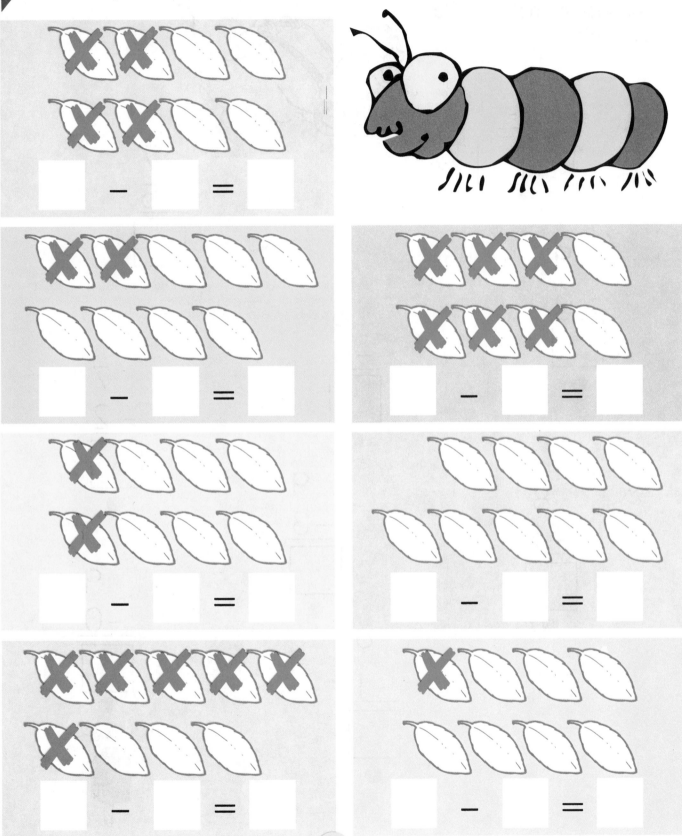

Beginning Subtraction Facts • LL 6929

Baby Bear's Treat

▶ Help Baby Bear find the way.
Connect the dots in order.
Start at **1**.

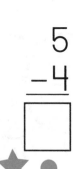

$$\begin{array}{r} 5 \\ -4 \\ \hline \end{array}$$
★ ●

$$\begin{array}{r} 7 \\ -5 \\ \hline \end{array}$$
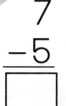
●

$$\begin{array}{r} 9 \\ -6 \\ \hline \end{array}$$
●

$$\begin{array}{r} 8 \\ -4 \\ \hline \end{array}$$
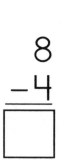
●

$$\begin{array}{r} 7 \\ -2 \\ \hline \end{array}$$

●

$$\begin{array}{r} 8 \\ -1 \\ \hline \end{array}$$

●

$$\begin{array}{r} 9 \\ -3 \\ \hline \end{array}$$
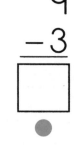
●

$$\begin{array}{r} 9 \\ -0 \\ \hline \end{array}$$
●

$$\begin{array}{r} 9 \\ -1 \\ \hline \end{array}$$
●

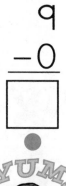

▶ **Can you find this "key" in the zoo?**

8 −3 5	4 −1	6 −2	9 −3	8 −0	7 −6
m					

1 – y
2 – t
3 – o
4 – n
5 – m
6 – k
7 – j
8 – e
9 – d
10 – a

Draw it here.

Hearts

▶ Show two problems for each picture.

 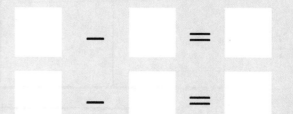

$$4 - 3 = 1$$
$$4 - 1 = 3$$

$$\square - \square = \square$$
$$\square - \square = \square$$

$$\square - \square = \square$$
$$\square - \square = \square$$

 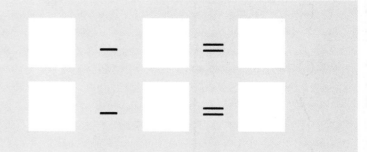

$$\square - \square = \square$$
$$\square - \square = \square$$

$$\square - \square = \square$$
$$\square - \square = \square$$

Beginning Subtraction Facts • LL 6929

▶ **Find the difference.**

8 – 6 = ☐   9 – 4 = ☐

8 – 4 = ☐   9 – 6 = ☐

8 – 7 = ☐   9 – 2 = ☐

8 – 3 = ☐   9 – 7 = ☐

8 – 8 = ☐   9 – 8 = ☐

8 – 1 = ☐   9 – 5 = ☐

8 – 2 = ☐   9 – 3 = ☐

8 – 5 = ☐   9 – 1 = ☐

9	8	8	9	9
-3	-6	-2	-5	-8
☐	☐	☐	☐	☐

8	8	9	8	9
-4	-2	-1	-7	-4
☐	☐	☐	☐	☐

Hidden Letter

Write the answers in the boxes.
Color all the answers **less than 5** blue.
Color all the answers **more than 5** red.

$9 - 0 = \square$	$7 - 6 = \square$	$8 - 1 = \square$
$9 - 3 = \square$	$9 - 9 = \square$	$9 - 1 = \square$
$8 - 0 = \square$	$6 - 0 = \square$	$7 - 1 = \square$
$8 - 2 = \square$	$7 - 3 = \square$	$9 - 0 = \square$
$9 - 2 = \square$	$8 - 5 = \square$	$9 - 3 = \square$

What letter in the alphabet do you see? _____

What has 4 wheels and flies?

$$\begin{array}{r} 6 \\ -5 \\ \hline \end{array}$$

$\begin{array}{r}9\\-7\\\hline\end{array}$	$\begin{array}{r}8\\-7\\\hline\end{array}$	$\begin{array}{r}6\\-3\\\hline\end{array}$	$\begin{array}{r}9\\-5\\\hline\end{array}$	$\begin{array}{r}3\\-2\\\hline\end{array}$	$\begin{array}{r}4\\-2\\\hline\end{array}$	$\begin{array}{r}9\\-4\\\hline\end{array}$

$\begin{array}{r}7\\-1\\\hline\end{array}$	$\begin{array}{r}8\\-5\\\hline\end{array}$	$\begin{array}{r}9\\-2\\\hline\end{array}$	$\begin{array}{r}9\\-1\\\hline\end{array}$	$\begin{array}{r}9\\-0\\\hline\end{array}$

1 – a	4 – b	7 – u
2 – g	5 – e	8 – c
3 – r	6 – t	9 – k

Find the Patterns

▶ Write the answer in the box.

9 − 9 = ☐   1 − 0 = ☐

7 − 7 = ☐   7 − 0 = ☐

3 − 3 = ☐   2 − 0 = ☐

5 − 5 = ☐   9 − 0 = ☐

8 − 8 = ☐   8 − 0 = ☐

1 − 1 = ☐   6 − 0 = ☐

4 − 4 = ☐   3 − 0 = ☐

2 − 2 = ☐   5 − 0 = ☐

6 − 6 = ☐   4 − 0 = ☐

▶ What are the rules?

_____   _____

_____   _____

▶ Write one less.

8	9	☐	4	☐	1	☐	5
☐	3	☐	8	☐	6	☐	2

▶ Take one away.

9	6	5	2
−1	−1	−1	−1
☐	☐	☐	☐

8	4	7	3
−1	−1	−1	−1
☐	☐	☐	☐

What's My Name?

▶ Write the numbers.
Follow the code to find my name.

9 −2	7 −3	9 −6	9 −8	5 −0
☐	☐	☐	☐	☐

9 −3	9 −7	7 −6	8 −3
☐	☐	☐	☐

1 – a	2 – e	3 – l
4 – o	5 – r	6 – b
7 – p		

▶ Draw a line to the answer.

9 – 5	2
7 – 1	6
6 – 4	4
5 – 2	3

8 – 0	3
6 – 2	4
9 – 6	5
7 – 2	8

7 – 1	2
9 – 7	5
8 – 3	3
6 – 3	6

9 – 8	1
7 – 4	2
4 – 2	5
6 – 1	3

9 – 4	2
7 – 0	5
8 – 6	7
5 – 2	3

8 – 5	5
9 – 1	8
7 – 2	0
6 – 6	3

Beginning Subtraction Facts • LL 6929

What's Missing?

▶ Write the number in the box.

3 + [2] = 5   [ ] + 2 = 8

[ ] + 4 = 7   6 + [ ] = 9

4 + [ ] = 10   [ ] + 8 = 12

[ ] + 3 = 6   4 + [ ] = 8

3 + [ ] = 8   [ ] + 5 = 9

[ ] + 2 = 4   4 + [ ] = 6

8 + [ ] = 9   [ ] + 1 = 4

[ ] + 5 = 7   3 + [ ] = 10

1 + [ ] = 5   [ ] + 5 = 6

Beginning Subtraction Facts • LL 6929

Subtract to Check Addition

▶ Find the answers.

3 +4 **7**	7 −3 4 7 −4 3

1 +3 **4**	4 −1 3 4 −3 1

2 +7 	___ ___

4 +2 	___ ___

7 +1 	___ ___

3 +5 	___ ___

6 +3 	___ ___

2 +6 	___ ___

Beginning Subtraction Facts • LL 6929

Help!

► Help the bird find her baby.

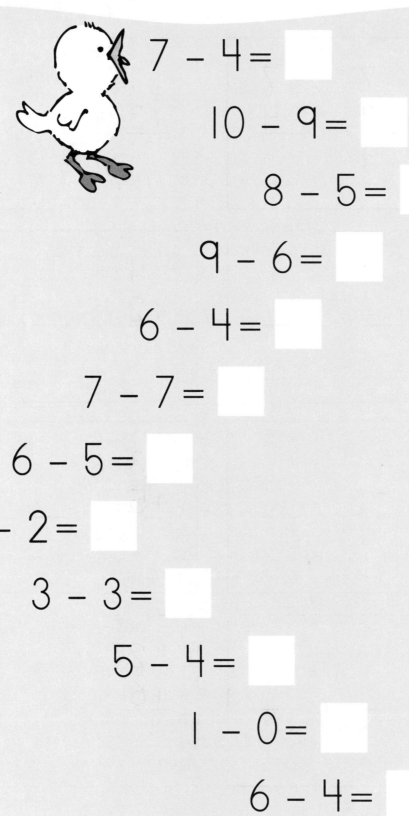

$7 - 4 = \boxed{}$

$10 - 9 = \boxed{}$

$8 - 5 = \boxed{}$

$9 - 6 = \boxed{}$

$6 - 4 = \boxed{}$

$7 - 7 = \boxed{}$

$6 - 5 = \boxed{}$

$9 - 2 = \boxed{}$

$3 - 3 = \boxed{}$

$5 - 4 = \boxed{}$

$1 - 0 = \boxed{}$

$6 - 4 = \boxed{}$

Beginning Subtraction Facts • LL 6929

Write the numbers.

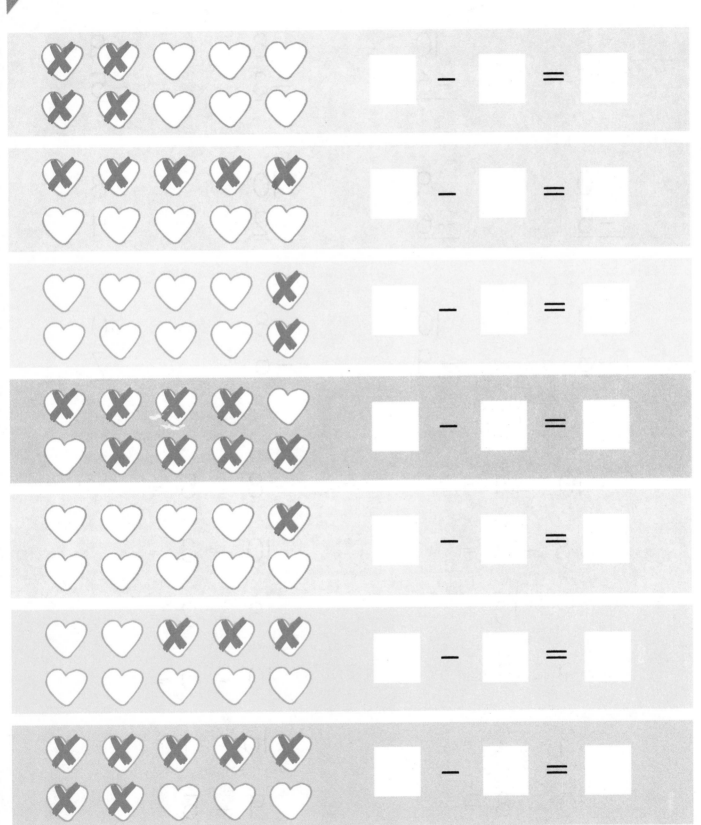

Practice Time

▶ Find the answers.

8 −5	10 −6	8 −3	9 −5
10 −5	9 −6	10 −2	8 −4
9 −3	10 −9	8 −6	10 −7

$10 - 4 =$ ☐ $8 - 5 =$ ☐

$8 - 1 =$ ☐ $10 - 3 =$ ☐

$10 - 10 =$ ☐ $8 - 2 =$ ☐

$9 - 7 =$ ☐ $10 - 0 =$ ☐

$9 - 2 =$ ☐ $10 - 1 =$ ☐

$10 - 8 =$ ☐ $9 - 5 =$ ☐

▶ Put the birds in their houses.

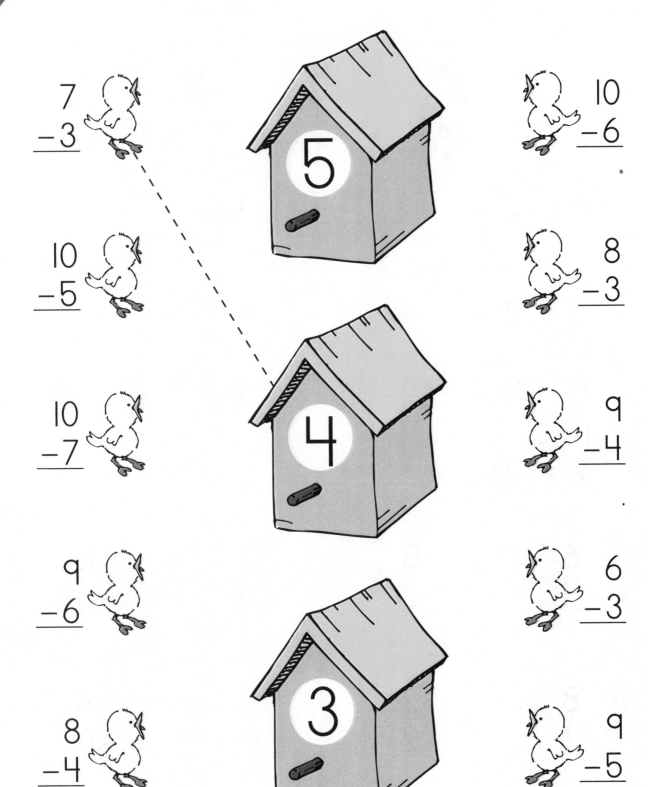

$$\begin{array}{r} 7 \\ -3 \\ \hline \end{array}$$

$$\begin{array}{r} 10 \\ -5 \\ \hline \end{array}$$

$$\begin{array}{r} 10 \\ -7 \\ \hline \end{array}$$

$$\begin{array}{r} 9 \\ -6 \\ \hline \end{array}$$

$$\begin{array}{r} 8 \\ -4 \\ \hline \end{array}$$

5

4

3

$$\begin{array}{r} 10 \\ -6 \\ \hline \end{array}$$

$$\begin{array}{r} 8 \\ -3 \\ \hline \end{array}$$

$$\begin{array}{r} 9 \\ -4 \\ \hline \end{array}$$

$$\begin{array}{r} 6 \\ -3 \\ \hline \end{array}$$

$$\begin{array}{r} 9 \\ -5 \\ \hline \end{array}$$

Beginning Subtraction Facts • LL 6929

Can you do all of these?

6 − 2 = ▢

4 − 1 = ▢

3 − 2 = ▢

4 − 0 = ▢

5 − 4 = ▢

3 − 1 = ▢

2 − 2 = ▢

5 − 2 = ▢

6	5	7	6
−4	−3	−0	−6
▢	▢	▢	▢

8	2	4	9
−1	−2	−4	−0
▢	▢	▢	▢

Beginning Subtraction Facts • LL 6929

▶ **Follow the directions.**

Color 5 blue.
Color 3 red.
Color 2 yellow.

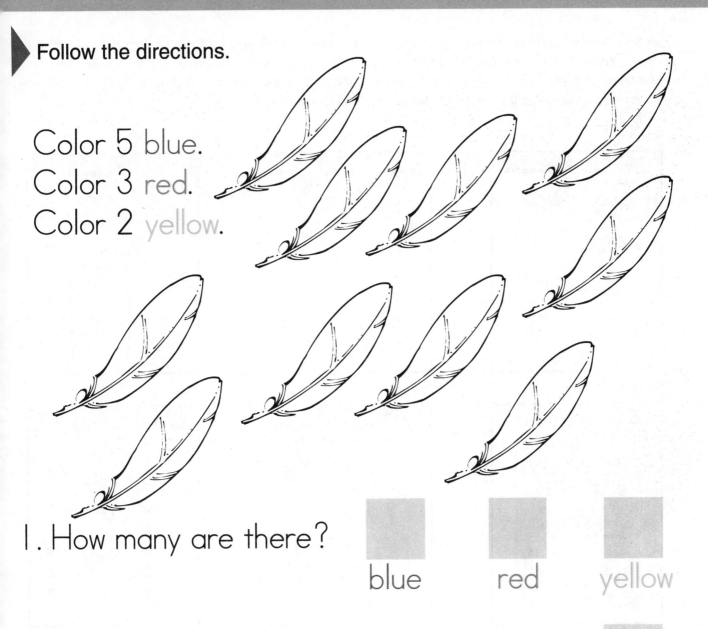

1. How many are there?

blue	red	yellow

2. How many more blue than yellow?

3. How many more red than yellow?

4. If 3 feathers flew away, how many would you have?

Answer Key

Please take time to go over the work your child has completed. Ask your child to explain what he or she has done. Praise both success and effort. If mistakes have been made, explain what the answer should have been and how to find it. Let your child know that mistakes are a part of learning. The time you spend with your child helps let him or her know you feel learning is important.

Page 1

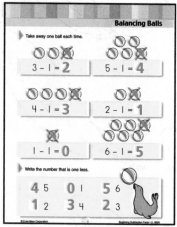

Balancing Balls

Take away one ball each time.

$3 - 1 = 2$ $5 - 1 = 4$

$4 - 1 = 3$ $2 - 1 = 1$

$1 - 1 = 0$ $6 - 1 = 5$

Write the number that is one less.

4 5   0 1   5 6
1 2   3 4   2 3

Page 2

Otter Do It

How many are left?

$5 - 2 = 3$

$4 - 1 = 3$

$3 - 2 = 1$

$4 - 2 = 2$

$5 - 0 = 5$

Page 3

Dinosaur Subtraction

Find the answer.

$5 - 1 = 4$

$5 - 5 = 0$ $5 - 3 = 2$
$4 - 1 = 3$ $4 - 2 = 2$
$4 - 2 = 2$ $2 - 0 = 2$
$3 - 3 = 0$ $3 - 2 = 1$
$2 - 1 = 1$ $5 - 4 = 1$
$4 - 0 = 4$ $3 - 1 = 2$

Page 4

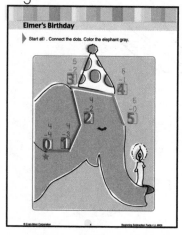

Elmer's Birthday

Start at 0. Connect the dots. Color the elephant gray.

Page 5

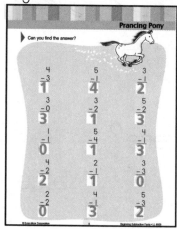

Prancing Pony

Can you find the answer?

$4 - 3 = 1$	$5 - 1 = 4$	$3 - 1 = 2$
$3 - 0 = 3$	$3 - 2 = 1$	$5 - 2 = 3$
$1 - 1 = 0$	$5 - 4 = 1$	$4 - 1 = 3$
$4 - 2 = 2$	$2 - 1 = 1$	$3 - 3 = 0$
$2 - 2 = 0$	$4 - 1 = 3$	$5 - 3 = 2$

Page 6

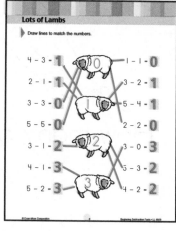

Lots of Lambs

Draw lines to match the numbers.

$4 - 3 = 1$ $1 - 1 = 0$
$2 - 1 = 1$ $3 - 2 = 1$
$3 - 3 = 0$ $5 - 4 = 1$
$5 - 5 = 0$ $2 - 2 = 0$
$3 - 1 = 2$ $3 - 0 = 3$
$4 - 1 = 3$ $5 - 3 = 2$
$5 - 2 = 3$ $4 - 2 = 2$

Page 7

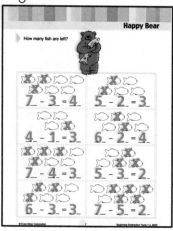

Happy Bear

How many fish are left?

$7 - 3 = 4$ $5 - 2 = 3$

$4 - 1 = 3$ $6 - 2 = 4$

$7 - 4 = 3$ $5 - 3 = 2$

$6 - 3 = 3$ $7 - 5 = 2$

Page 8

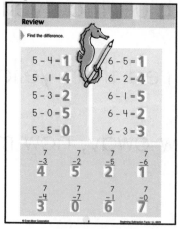

Review

Find the difference.

$5 - 4 = 1$ $6 - 5 = 1$
$5 - 1 = 4$ $6 - 2 = 4$
$5 - 3 = 2$ $6 - 1 = 5$
$5 - 0 = 5$ $6 - 4 = 2$
$5 - 5 = 0$ $6 - 3 = 3$

7	7	7	7
-3	-2	-5	-6
4	5	2	1

7	7	7	7
-4	-7	-1	-0
3	0	6	7

Page 9

Ant Subtraction

How fast can you find the answer?

7	2	4	7	5
-4	-0	-2	-1	-2
3	2	2	6	3

6	5	5	7	2
-2	-3	-4	-6	-1
4	2	1	1	1

3	5	7	5	4
-1	-0	-2	-1	-4
2	5	5	4	0

5	6	4	3	6
-0	-6	-2	-2	-1
5	0	2	1	5

6	7	6	5	6
-5	-4	-4	-3	-1
1	3	2	2	5

Beginning Subtraction Facts • LL 6929

Page 10

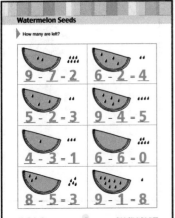

Watermelon Seeds

How many are left?

9 − 7 = 2
6 − 2 = 4
5 − 2 = 3
9 − 4 = 5
4 − 3 = 1
6 − 6 = 0
8 − 5 = 3
9 − 1 = 8

Page 11

Hungry Caterpillar

How many did I eat?

8 − 4 = 4
9 − 2 = 7
8 − 6 = 2
8 − 2 = 6
9 − 0 = 9
9 − 6 = 3
8 − 1 = 7

Page 12

Baby Bear's Treat

Help Baby Bear find the way. Connect the dots in order. Start at 1.

5 − 4 = 1
7 − 5 = 2
9 − 6 = 3
8 − 4 = 4
7 − 2 = 5
9 − 3 = 6
8 − 1 = 7
8 − 0 = 8
9 − 0 = 9

Page 13

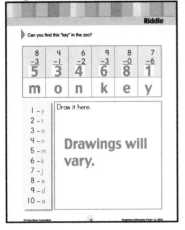

Riddle

Can you find this "key" in the zoo?

8 −3 = 5	4 −1 = 3	6 −2 = 4	9 −3 = 6	8 −0 = 8	7 −6 = 1
m	o	n	k	e	y

1 − y
2 − t
3 − o
4 − n
5 − m
6 − k
7 − j
8 − e
9 − d
10 − a

Draw it here.

Drawings will vary.

Page 14

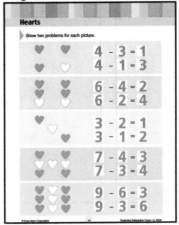

Hearts

Show two problems for each picture.

4 − 3 = 1
4 − 1 = 3

6 − 4 = 2
6 − 2 = 4

3 − 2 = 1
3 − 1 = 2

7 − 4 = 3
7 − 3 = 4

9 − 6 = 3
9 − 3 = 6

Page 15

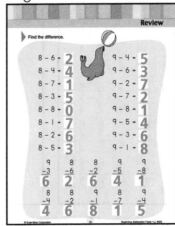

Review

Find the difference.

8 − 6 = 2   9 − 4 = 5
8 − 4 = 4   9 − 6 = 3
8 − 7 = 1   9 − 2 = 7
8 − 3 = 5   9 − 7 = 2
8 − 8 = 0   9 − 8 = 1
8 − 1 = 7   9 − 5 = 4
8 − 2 = 6   9 − 3 = 6
8 − 5 = 3   9 − 1 = 8

9 −3 = 6
8 −6 = 2
8 −2 = 6
9 −5 = 4
9 −8 = 1
8 −4 = 4
8 −2 = 6
9 −1 = 8
8 −7 = 1
9 −4 = 5

Page 16

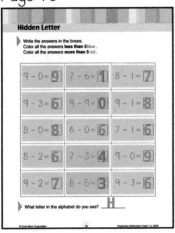

Hidden Letter

Write the answers in the boxes.
Color all the answers **less than 5** blue.
Color all the answers **more than 5** red.

9 − 0 = 9   7 − 6 = 1   8 − 1 = 7
9 − 3 = 6   9 − 9 = 0   9 − 1 = 8
8 − 0 = 8   6 − 0 = 6   7 − 1 = 6
8 − 2 = 6   7 − 3 = 4   9 − 0 = 9
9 − 2 = 7   8 − 5 = 3   9 − 3 = 6

What letter in the alphabet do you see? **H**

Page 17

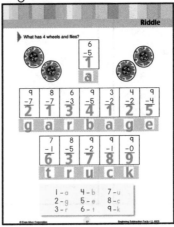

Riddle

What has 4 wheels and flies?

6 −5 = 1
a

9 −7 =2	8 −7 =1	6 −3 =3	3 −2 =1	4 −3 =1	9 −4 =5
g	a	r	b	a	g	e

7 −1 =6	8 −5 =3	9 −2 =7	9 −1 =8	9 −0 =9
t	r	u	c	k

1 − a   4 − b   7 − u
2 − r   5 − e   8 − c
3 − r   6 − t   9 − k

Page 18

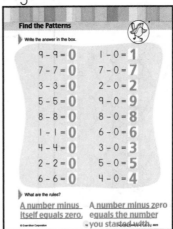

Find the Patterns

Write the answer in the box.

9 − 9 = 0   1 − 0 = 1
7 − 7 = 0   7 − 0 = 7
3 − 3 = 0   2 − 0 = 2
5 − 5 = 0   9 − 0 = 9
8 − 8 = 0   8 − 0 = 8
1 − 1 = 0   6 − 0 = 6
4 − 4 = 0   3 − 0 = 3
2 − 2 = 0   5 − 0 = 5
6 − 6 = 0   4 − 0 = 4

What are the rules?

A number minus itself equals zero.   A number minus zero equals the number you started with.

Page 19

Test Yourself

Write one less.

8 9   3 4   0 1   4 5

2 3   7 8   5 6   1 2

Take one away.

$9 - 1 = 8$ $6 - 1 = 5$ $5 - 1 = 4$ $2 - 1 = 1$

$8 - 1 = 7$ $4 - 1 = 3$ $7 - 1 = 6$ $3 - 1 = 2$

Page 20

What's My Name?

Write the numbers.
Follow the code to find my name.

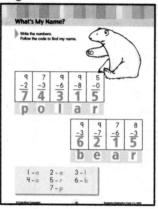

$9-2$	$7-3$	$9-6$	$8-5$	$9-0$
7	4	3	1	5
p	o	l	a	r

$9-3$	$9-7$	$7-6$	$8-3$
6	2	1	5
b	e	a	r

1 – o   2 – e   3 – l
4 – a   5 – r   6 – b
7 – p

Page 21

Make a Match

Draw a line to the answer.

$9-5$ ... 2 $8-0$ ... 3
$7-1$ ... 6 $6-2$ ... 4
$6-4$ ... 9 $9-6$ ... 2
$5-2$ ... 3 $7-2$ ... 8

$7-1$ ... 6 $9-8$ ... 1
$9-7$ ... 5 $7-4$ ... 3
$8-3$ ... 4 $4-2$ ... 2
$6-3$ ... 3 $6-1$ ... 5

$9-4$ ... 2 $8-5$ ... 5
$7-0$ ... 7 $9-1$ ... 8
$8-6$ ... 5 $7-2$ ... 0
$5-2$ ... 2 $6-6$ ... 3

Page 22

What's Missing?

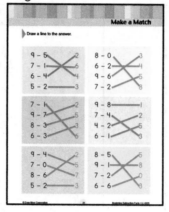

Write the number in the box.

$3 + 2 = 5$ $6 + 2 = 8$
$3 + 4 = 7$ $6 + 3 = 9$
$4 + 6 = 10$ $4 + 8 = 12$
$3 + 3 = 6$ $4 + 4 = 8$
$3 + 5 = 8$ $4 + 5 = 9$
$2 + 2 = 4$ $4 + 2 = 6$
$8 + 1 = 9$ $3 + 1 = 4$
$2 + 5 = 7$ $3 + 7 = 10$
$1 + 4 = 5$ $1 + 5 = 6$

Page 23

Subtract to Check Addition

Find the answers.

$3 + 4 = 7$ $7 - 3 = 4$ $7 - 4 = 3$ $4 + 4 = 4$ $4 - 1 = 3$ $4 - 3 = 1$

$2 + 7 = 9$ $9 - 2 = 7$ $9 - 7 = 2$ $4 + 2 = 6$ $6 - 4 = 2$ $6 - 2 = 4$

$7 + 1 = 8$ $8 - 1 = 7$ $8 - 7 = 1$ $3 + 5 = 8$ $8 - 3 = 5$ $8 - 5 = 3$

$6 + 3 = 9$ $9 - 6 = 3$ $9 - 3 = 6$ $2 + 6 = 8$ $8 - 2 = 6$ $8 - 6 = 2$

Page 24

Help!

Help the bird find her baby.

$7 - 4 = 3$
$10 - 9 = 1$
$8 - 5 = 3$
$9 - 6 = 3$
$6 - 4 = 2$
$7 - 7 = 0$
$6 - 5 = 1$
$9 - 2 = 7$
$3 - 3 = 0$
$5 - 4 = 1$
$1 - 0 = 1$
$6 - 4 = 2$

Page 25

Start with 10

Write the numbers.

$10 - 4 = 6$
$10 - 5 = 5$
$10 - 2 = 8$
$10 - 8 = 2$
$10 - 1 = 9$
$10 - 3 = 7$
$10 - 7 = 3$

Page 26

Practice Time

Find the answers.

$8 - 5 = 3$ $10 - 6 = 4$ $8 - 3 = 5$ $9 - 5 = 4$

$10 - 5 = 5$ $9 - 6 = 3$ $10 - 2 = 8$ $8 - 4 = 4$

$9 - 3 = 6$ $10 - 9 = 1$ $8 - 6 = 2$ $10 - 7 = 3$

$10 - 4 = 6$ $8 - 5 = 3$
$8 - 1 = 7$ $10 - 3 = 7$
$10 - 10 = 0$ $8 - 2 = 6$
$9 - 7 = 2$ $10 - 0 = 10$
$9 - 2 = 7$ $10 - 1 = 9$
$10 - 8 = 2$ $9 - 5 = 4$

Page 27

Fly Away Home

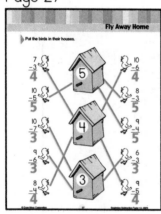

Put the birds in their houses.

$7 - 3 = 4$ $10 - 6 = 4$

$10 - 5 = 5$ $8 - 3 = 5$

house: 5

$10 - 7 = 3$ $9 - 4 = 5$

house: 4

$9 - 6 = 3$ $6 - 3 = 3$

house: 3

$8 - 4 = 4$ $9 - 5 = 4$

Page 28

Review

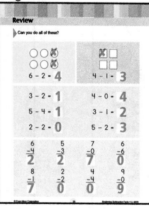

Can you do all of these?

$6 - 2 = 4$ $4 - 1 = 3$

$3 - 2 = 1$ $4 - 0 = 4$
$5 - 4 = 1$ $3 - 1 = 2$
$2 - 2 = 0$ $5 - 2 = 3$

$6 - 4 = 2$ $5 - 3 = 2$ $7 - 0 = 7$ $6 - 6 = 0$

$8 - 1 = 7$ $2 - 2 = 0$ $4 - 4 = 0$ $9 - 0 = 9$

Page 29

Feather the Nest

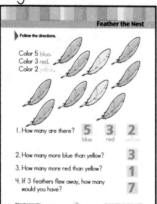

Follow the directions.

Color 5 blue.
Color 3 red.
Color 2 yellow.

1. How many are there?   5 blue   3 red   2 yellow

2. How many more blue than yellow?   3

3. How many more red than yellow?   1

4. If 3 feathers flew away, how many would you have?   7